GRUESOME GRUB
Halloween Party Recipes & Pumpkin Patterns

Executive Producers: Kim Mitzo Thompson, Karen Mitzo Hilderbrand
Audio Track Programming: David Paglisotti
Author: Ken Carder
Book Design: Matthew Van Zomeren
Pumpkin Carving Patterns: David Schimmell

Twin Sisters Productions
4710 Hudson Drive
Stow, OH 44224 USA
www.twinsisters.com
1-800-248-8946

Bug Blood

Thirsting for something really creepy?

You'll need:
- Two 10-oz packages of frozen strawberries, defrosted
- One 6-oz can of lemonade concentrate, thawed
- One quart of ginger ale
- Two Cups of raisins

Mix the strawberries and lemonade concentrate in a blender until smooth and thick. Slowly add ginger ale to the strawberry-lemonade mixture. Pour the drink into a punch bowl, then stir in the raisins and pretend they're tasty "floating bugs!"

Boiling Witch's Cauldron

You'll need:
- A plastic witch's cauldron from your nearest Halloween supply store
- Frozen lemonade or other drink mix
- 2 Two-liter lemon-lime or ginger ale sodas
- Cut up fresh fruit: watermelon, strawberries, melons, oranges, grapes
- Grape powdered drink mix
- Optional: plastic bones, spiders, bats
- Optional: dry ice—used only with adult supervision

In the clean plastic witch's cauldron, prepare the frozen drink mix according to package instructions. Add the lemon-lime soda or ginger ale. Add the cut-up fruit. Darken the mixture with grape powdered drink mix. For added effect, add plastic bones, eyeballs, bats, spiders or other ghoulish toys. Only with adult supervision, add dry ice for the boiling effect and to have "steam" rolling over the edges. Remove the dry ice before serving.

Slime Juice

You'll need:
- 6-oz package of blue powdered drink mix
- 12-oz can orange juice concentrate
- 1-gallon water

Mix together the orange juice and powdered drink mix, add water, stir and watch the beverage turn green.

Here is another tasty disgusting option:

You'll need:
- 2 packages of lime gelatin (3-oz size)
- 1-½ Cups water, boiling
- 6-oz frozen Limeade
- 2 Cups water
- Green food coloring
- 10-oz Club soda or carbonated water

Prepare the lime gelatin according to the package directions. Carefully pour the mixture into a 9-inch square pan and chill about three hours, until firm. In a large pitcher, combine the limeade, remaining water and food coloring to turn the drink bright green. Chill the drink. When the gelatin is set, cut out strips or small shapes using cookie cutters. To serve, add club soda or carbonated water to the limeade and pour over ice. Put a lime gelatin shape in each glass.

Spider Guts Cake

Slice into this gooey cake for a disgusting surprise!

You'll need:
- 1 Basic cake mix
- 1 Package of green gelatin, prepared according to package directions
- Black frosting–available at craft supply stores or make your own by adding blue food coloring to chocolate frosting
- Black licorice sticks or whips
- Large green gumdrops

Mix the cake batter according to package directions. Bake it in two metal bowls —one bowl larger than the other. Once the cakes have baked and cooled, remove them from the mold. To make the spider's body, cut the larger cake in half horizontally. Scoop out a hole in each half. Fill the hole with the green gelatin. Put both halves of the larger cake back together. Frost it black and arrange on a serving platter, adding the legs and eyes. When the cake is cut into, it will ooze green guts!

Gruesome Brew

A spicy hot drink to warm little goblins.

You'll need:
- ½-cup lemon juice
- 1 Quart apple cider
- 5 Cloves
- 1 teaspoon nutmeg
- 2 Cinnamon sticks

Mix lemon juice and cider in a saucepan. Put the cloves, nutmeg and cinnamon in a tea ball and add to cider. Bring the mixture to a boil over low heat and simmer for 5-10 minutes. Cool slightly, remove tea ball, and serve. The brew may also be served cold.

Green Eye Pie

How many eyes are in this pie?

You'll need:
- Green grapes
- Whipped topping or sour cream
- Prepared graham cracker pie crust
- 2 Tablespoons brown sugar

In a bowl combine 2 cups of washed and dried green grapes and ½-cup of whipped topping (or sour cream). Pour into the prepared graham cracker pie crust. Chill. Sprinkle with brown sugar before serving.

Sewer Slurpies

Disgusting? Yes, but a tasty ice cream slurpy beverage!

You'll need:
- Chocolate chip ice cream
- Chocolate syrup
- Club soda
- Large glasses
- Straws
- Spoons

Let the ice cream sit at room temperature until it's easy to scoop. Fill tall glasses about half full with the ice cream goop. Squeeze several tablespoons of chocolate syrup into each glass. Slowly fill glasses with club soda and serve with a straw and long spoon.

RECIPES

Egg Eyeballs

So you're not a brain surgeon! How about an eye doctor with eye-popping treats?

You'll need:
- 6 Eggs, hard-cooked, cooled and peeled
- 6-oz container of whipped cream cheese
- 12 Green olives stuffed with pimientos
- Ketchup

Cut the eggs in half widthwise. Remove the yolks and fill the hole with cream cheese.

Press an olive into each cream cheese eyeball, pimiento up, for an eerie green iris and red pupil. Dip a toothpick into ketchup and draw broken blood vessels in the cream cheese!

Chocolate-Covered Bugs

Tasty little insects are so much fun!

You'll need:
- Red-licorice whips
- Soft caramel candies
- Chocolate chips
- Optional: Colored sprinkles, candies, coconut sliced Almonds
- Baking sheet
- Waxed Paper

First, cut the licorice whips into small pieces and set them aside. Unwrap the caramels and flatten each one into a small oval with your hands. Press the small pieces of licorice onto each of the flattened caramels to make bug legs. Top each bug with a second caramel and seal together by pressing the edges. Put each bug on a baking sheet lined with waxed paper.

Melt the chocolate chips in a microwave-safe bowl. Microwave on High about 1 minute. Stir. Then microwave on High 1 minute longer. Remove the chocolate from the microwave and stir until melted. Spoon melted chocolate over each candy. Decorate the bugs with nuts, candies, sprinkles, or coconut.

Kitty Litter Cake

Imagine serving invited guests your kitty's dirty litter for dessert!

You'll need
- 1 Spice cake mix
- 1 White cake mix
- 1 Package of white sandwich cookies
- Green food coloring
- 12 Small, rounded chocolate stick rolls
- 1 Package vanilla pudding mix
- 1 New kitty litter box
- 1 New "Pooper Scooper" utensil

Prepare the cake mixes and bake according to the package directions. Prepare the pudding mix and chill until ready to assemble. Crumble white sandwich cookies in small batches in blender. Set aside all but about ½-cup. Add a few drops green food coloring to the ½-cup of cookie crumbs, and mix using a fork. When cooled to room temperature, crumble both cakes into a large bowl. Toss with half the remaining cookie crumbs and the chilled pudding. Gently combine. Line new, clean kitty litter box with plastic wrap. Spread the cake and cookie mixture into the litter box. Heat several unwrapped rounded chocolate stick rolls in a microwave safe dish until soft and pliable. Shape the ends of the chocolate so they are no longer blunt, curving slightly. Bury the chocolate treats in the "litter" mixture. Sprinkle the other half of cookie crumbs over top. Scatter the green cookie crumbs lightly over the top—to represent the chlorophyll in kitty litter. Heat remaining chocolate stick rolls in the microwave until almost melted. Scrape them on top of the cake and sprinkle with cookie crumbs. Serve the dessert with a new "Pooper Scooper"—the small shovel-like utensil used for sifting kitty litter.

Bone Bread

And just where did these fresh bones come from?

You'll need:
- Refrigerated bread dough
- Coarse sea salt

Unroll a tube of refrigerated bread dough. Separate the rectangular pieces. Stretch one piece of dough. Carefully cut a slit in the center of each end. Roll and shape the four flaps of dough into knobs that look like the ends of a bone. Repeat with the remaining rectangular pieces of dough. Place the dough bones on an ungreased baking sheet. Sprinkle the bones with coarse sea salt and bake until they are light golden brown.

Monstermallows

Frightfully fun treats to eat and to share!

You'll need:
- Marshmallows
- Green food coloring paste
- Chocolate chips
- Small round candies for eyes
- Thin pretzel sticks
- Craft sticks
- New paintbrushes
- Foam cups

Insert a craft stick up through the bottom of a marshmallow so that the marshmallow rests on top of the stick forming a "head". Paint the entire marshmallow green with the green food coloring paste. In a microwave safe bowl, melt the chocolate chips. Dip the top of the marshmallow into the chocolate to create his "hair".

Insert the sticks into the bottom of a foam cup. Place the cup and marshmallow stick into the refrigerator for few minutes to harden the chocolate. Next, dip two round candies into the melted chocolate and "glue" them to the head for eyes. Paint on a chocolate mouth. Break off the ends of a pretzel stick. Poke one piece into each side of the monster's head. Wrap each Monstermallow in cellophane or plastic wrap to give away as treats.

Worms In The Mud

Eat dirt? Eat worms? Sure you can—with this tasty chocolate pudding treat.

You'll need:
- Instant chocolate pudding mix
- Gummy worms
- Chocolate graham crackers

Follow the directions on the box of the pudding mix; make sure you stir it enough to get rid of the lumps. Put it in the refrigerator to set. When the pudding is set, crumble up some graham crackers and mix them into the pudding. Next, stir in some gummy worms, making sure they are covered in pudding. Divide the pudding into four dishes, crumble some more graham crackers on top, and add a couple of worms!

RECIPES

Skull Cakes

Serve these long-lost human skulls to your guests!

You'll need:
- Cupcakes in liners
- Marshmallows
- White frosting
- Mints
- Chocolate chips
- Slivered almonds

Cut the marshmallows in half. (Kitchen shears dipped in confectioner's sugar keeps the marshmallows from sticking.) Pull each cupcake liner away and tuck half a marshmallow between the paper and the cupcake. Frost the cupcake and marshmallow to create a skull. Add mints or chocolate chips for eyes. Use slivered almonds for teeth.

Boogers on a Stick

The name says it all! Kids will love them!

You'll need:
- 8-oz jar of processed cheese spread
- 3 or 4 drops green food coloring
- 3 dozen pretzel sticks

Melt the processed cheese spread in the microwave according to jar directions. Allow the cheese to cool slightly in the jar. Carefully stir in food coloring using just enough to turn the cheese a pale, snot green color. To form boogers: Dip and twist the tip of each pretzel stick into the cheese, lift out, wait twenty seconds, then dip again. When cheese lumps reach a boogerish size, set boogered pretzels on wax paper to cool.

Dead Finger Cookies

Cookies give new meaning to the term "finger food."

You'll need:
- Cookie dough
- Almonds

Put refrigerated sugar cookie dough in a large plastic storage bag. Cut a "finger-size" corner off the bag. Carefully squeeze finger-length dough onto a cookie sheet. Use a dull side of butter knife to carve lines into each finger—knuckles and wrinkles. Use an almond to make a fingernail impression at the tip of each finger cookie. Bake the cookies according to the package directions. After baking, "glue" an almond to each finger.

Chopped Off Fingers Pizza

Make the next homemade pizza one to remember with these misplaced fingertips.

You'll need:
- 1 Red bell pepper
- Mozzarella sticks
- Baked pizza crusts
- Pizza sauce

Core, stem and seed, and cut a red pepper lengthwise into 1-inch wide strips. Cut each strip crosswise into ½-inch pieces. Trim one end to make the fingernails.

Make fingers by cutting each cheese stick in half crosswise. Cut out a ½-inch square notch on the rounded end of each "finger" into which a pepper piece will fit to make a fingernail.

Prepare your homemade pizza crust, sauce, and toppings. Lay several cheese fingers well apart on the crust. Place a red pepper fingernail onto each. Bake as directed.

Simple Pimples

Go ahead and squeeze these pimples!

You'll need:
- 1-2 dozen cherry tomatoes
- Flavored soft cream cheese spread

Core each tomato with a carrot peeler or small kitchen knife. Drain excess tomato juice. Using a butter knife, fill holes in tomatoes with cream cheese. Gently squeeze each pimple and arrange on a platter.

Baked Eyeballs

Keep a close eye on these simple treats.

You'll need:
- Mashed potatoes
- Sliced black olives or round candies

Roll mashed potatoes into eyeball-sized balls. Bake them about 20 minutes in a 200° oven—until they are lightly brown and crunchy. Remove the eyeballs from the oven and carefully insert the pupil—sliced black olives or a colorful round candy.

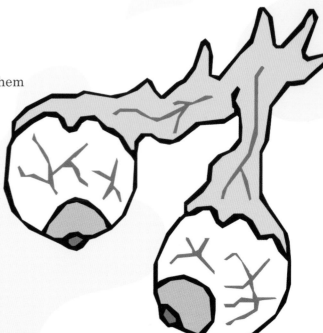

Bone Sandwiches

Who knew it was so easy to make human bones—complete with the marrow and blood!

You'll need:
- White bread
- Peanut butter
- Jelly

Cut the crusts off of several slices of white bread. Spread peanut butter and jelly on the bread. Roll the sandwiches up. You have bones with blood and marrow for dinner!

Miniature Tombstones

Your friends are certain to R.I.P. with these simple treats.

You'll need:
- Icing
- Square or rectangle shaped cookies or biscuits
- Water

In a small bowl add small amounts of hot water to the icing, until the mixture becomes fairly runny. Dip each cookie or biscuit into the mixture. Place the cookies onto a foiled tray. Use a toothpick to carve R.I.P. or some other epitaph into the icing. Place the tombstones in the refrigerator for several hours.

Frog's Eye Salad

Every little witch and goblin will savor this tasty treat.

You'll need:
- 1 Cup Acini De Pepe
    —very small round pasta balls
- 2 Cups mandarin oranges
- 1 Cup crushed pineapple
- 1-½ Cups miniature marshmallows
- 3 Egg yolks
- 1 Cup sugar
- 1 Tub of whipped topping

Cook the pasta according to the package instructions until tender, but not soft. Drain and rinse the pasta. Drain cans of pineapple and mandarin oranges, reserving the juice. Mix the juices, sugar, and egg yolks in a medium saucepan. Bring the mixture to a full boil. Pour the mixture over the pasta. Refrigerate the pasta overnight. When cooled, mix in the pineapple and oranges. Then fold in the whipped cream and marshmallows. Chill before serving.

Fruity, Skewered Eyeballs

Who knew eyeballs were so healthy?

You'll need:
- 6 Green grapes
- 6 Raisins
- ½-Cup whipped topping
- 6 Toothpicks
- Oranges

Carefully place a grape onto a toothpick, so that about 1/8-inch of the toothpick comes through the other side of the grape. Place a raisin on the exposed toothpick. Using the backside of a spoon, cover the grape with whipped topping for the "whites" of the eyes! To serve, slice an orange in half. Place the flat side down on a plate and stick the long end of toothpicks into the rind. Garnish the plate with loose grapes.

Barf Dip

Tasty and disgusting—a great combination!

You'll need:
- 1 Can of Black beans, drained
- 1 Can of corn, drained
- 1 Jar processed cheese spread
- Diced tomatoes
- Green onions, chopped
- Black olives, chopped
- Tortilla chips

In a microwave-safe bowl, mash ½ can of black beans. Add a small jar of processed cheese spread or cheese dip, some diced tomatoes, drained canned corn, green onions, a few chopped black olives, or any other ugly looking foods. Heat the mixture in the microwave for two or three minutes, stirring frequently. Serve the barf dip with tortilla chips or cut veggies.

Fried Spiders

Hot, crunchy munchies!

You'll need:
- 1 Frozen ready-to-bake breaded cream-cheese-filled jalapeno popper
- 4 Frozen ready-to-bake breaded onion rings
- Egg wash
- Wooden toothpicks soaked in water

Thaw the jalapeno poppers and onion rings slightly. Cut the onion rings in half to make the curved legs. Attach the 8 legs to the jalapeno pepper body with egg wash and hold in place with the wet toothpicks. Bake in the oven according to the jalapeno popper package instructions. Carefully arrange on a serving platter—removing the toothpicks.

Brain Bread

Adding Brain Bread to your diet will make you very smart!

You'll need:
- ½-Cup (1 stick) unsalted butter
- ½-Cup milk
- ½-Cup water
- 5 to 5-½ Cups all-purpose flour
- 2 Packages dry yeast
- 1 Teaspoon salt
- 1 Tablespoon whole anise seed
- 1 Cup sugar
- 4 Eggs
- ⅓-Cup freshly squeezed orange juice
- 2 Tablespoons grated orange zest

In a saucepan heat the butter, milk, and water until the butter melts. In a large mixing bowl, combine 1-½ cups of the flour, the yeast, salt and anise seed, and ½-cup of the sugar. Add the butter and milk mixture and stir until well combined. Add the eggs and beat in 1 cup of flour. Continue to add more flour until the dough is soft but not sticky. Knead the dough on a lightly floured board for 10 minutes, or until smooth and elastic. Lightly grease a large mixing bowl and place the dough in it. Cover with plastic wrap and let rise in a warm place until it doubles in size, about 1½ hours. Punch the dough down and shape into 2 loaves that look like a brain or skull. Allow the bread to rise in a warm place for 1 hour. Preheat the oven to 350° F. Bake the loaves on a baking sheet for 40 minutes, or until the tops are golden brown.

While the bread is baking, prepare the glaze. In a small saucepan, mix the remaining ½-cup of sugar, orange juice, and orange zest over high heat. Bring to a boil, stirring constantly, for two minutes, then remove from the heat. Keep warm. While the bread is hot, apply the warm glaze to the hot loaves with a pastry brush.

Worm Burgers

These aged, wormy burgers are certain to get a reaction from unsuspecting dinner guests!

You'll need:
- 1-½ Cups Bean Sprouts
- 1-lb Ground beef
- 1 Egg
- Salt and pepper to taste
- Mayonnaise, ketchup, mustard
- Hamburger buns

Wash the bean sprouts with warm water. Mix 1 cup of bean sprouts, ground beef and raw egg together in a bowl. Save the remaining sprouts until later. With adult help, form the burgers into patties, season, and cook them as usual. When they're cooked through, place each on an open bun and sprinkle the remaining "worms" on top. Don't forget the pus and blood on the side—ketchup, mustard, mayonnaise mixed together!

Cadaver Dip

Force your guests to do surgery with this frightening but tasty dip.

You'll need:
- Your favorite cheese dip—pliable for molding
- Very thinly sliced cooked ham
- Crackers

On a platter carefully shape your favorite cheese dip into the size and shape of a small human head. Sculpt a nose, lips, and recesses for the eyes. Next, carefully cover the entire sculpture with very thin—almost paper-like—slices of cooked ham. Serve the face dip with crackers.

Dinner in a Pumpkin

A delicious hot dish served in a real baked pumpkin!

You'll need:
- 1 Small to medium pumpkin
- 1 4-oz can sliced mushrooms, drained
- 1 Onion, chopped
- 1 10-oz can cream of chicken soup
- 2 Tablespoons vegetable oil
- 1 8-oz can sliced water chestnuts, drained
- 1-½ to 2 lbs ground beef
- 1-½ cups cooked rice
- 2 Tablespoons soy sauce
- 2 Tablespoons brown sugar

Cut off top of pumpkin and clean out the seeds and pulp. Draw an appropriate face on front of pumpkin with permanent marker. In a large skillet, sauté the onion in oil until tender; add meat and brown. Drain drippings from skillet. Add soy sauce, brown sugar, mushrooms and soup; simmer 10 minutes, stirring occasionally. Add cooked rice and water chestnuts. Spoon the mixture into pumpkin shell. Replace the pumpkin top and place entire pumpkin, with filling, on a baking sheet. Bake for 1 hour in 350° oven or until inside meat of pumpkin is tender. Put pumpkin on a plate; remove top and serve.

Cheesy Candy Corn

A hot and tasty take on the traditional Halloween candy.

You'll need:
- Small, round prebaked pizza crusts
- Variety of sliced cheeses: Mozzarella, Provolone, Monterey Jack, Cheddar

Heat the oven to 450° F. Cut small round prebaked pizza crusts into wedges—the shape of a candy corn. Top each wedge with rows of white, orange, and yellow cheeses. Bake the wedges on a cookie sheet for 8 to 10 minutes. Allow the cheesy candy corns to cool for 5 minutes before serving.

Wormy Baked Apples

A perfect treat on a cold, damp Halloween night!

You'll need:
- 12 Large baking apples
- 8-oz Jar boysenberry or dark colored jam
- 4 Tablespoons butter
- 12 Gummy worm candies

Preheat oven to 350° F. Core apples from the stem end to ½-inch from the bottom. Do not push through. Stuff each hole with 1 teaspoon each of jam and butter. Place in a pan and bake uncovered for 35 to 45 minutes, depending on the size of the apples. Each apple should be tender but not mushy. Remove the apples from the oven and allow to cool 15 minutes. Place each apple in a bowl and spoon syrup from the baking pan around it. Insert a gummy worm in the top of each apple.

English Mummies

Imagine who might be behind these tasty wrappings!

You'll need:
- English muffins
- Pizza sauce
- Olive slices
- Green or red pepper pieces
- String cheese (pulled apart)

Split and toast an English muffin. Spread pizza sauce onto one half of the muffin. For eyes, place two olive slices topped with red or green pepper pieces. To make the mummy wrappings, lay strips of string cheese across the muffin. Bake at 350° for about 10 minutes, or until the cheese is melted.

Worms on a Bun

Hot dogs never looked so bad but tasted so good!

You'll need:
- Hot dogs
- Hamburger buns
- Ketchup

Cut the hot dogs into thin slices. Boil or microwave until the slices curl like wiggly worms. Serve three or four worms on a hamburger bun. Add a few squiggles of ketchup.

Mashed Potato Caterpillars

Caterpillars, maggots—you decide!

You'll need:
- 4 Cups prepared mashed potatoes (your favorite recipe or instant)
- Yellow liquid food coloring
- Red liquid food coloring
- Frozen vegetables: green beans, carrots, corn, peas
- Celery

In a medium mixing bowl, add yellow food coloring to the potatoes and stir to combine; add a few drops of red food coloring to the potatoes and stir again to mix the colors. Continue to add more red or yellow coloring to achieve the desired shade of orange. Using clean, damp hands form the potatoes into small balls, each about 1-_ inches in diameter. On microwave-safe plate, arrange 8 potato balls, side-by-side and overlapping each other slightly, to form curved caterpillar body. Insert green beans for legs on the sides of the caterpillar bodies. Decorate each caterpillar with additional vegetables: thawed frozen carrot cubes, kernels of corn, frozen peas for eyes, a slice of celery for a mouth. Reheat the caterpillars in the microwave and serve.

Scrambled Scarecrow

Serve guests what's left of your favorite Halloween scarecrow!

You'll need:
- 3 Cups small pretzels
- 3 Cups shoestring potatoes
- 3 Cups Spanish peanuts
- ½-Cup seasoned croutons
- 4-½ oz can French fried onions
- ½-Cup margarine
- ½-Cup Parmesan cheese

Mix all the ingredients in a large baking pan. Bake at 250 degrees for 1 hour, stirring often.

Vampire's Blood Shake

You'll need:
- 2 Cups plain yogurt
- ½-Teaspoon vanilla extract
- 1 Package frozen strawberries or raspberries, thawed
- Ice cubes
- 1 Pint strawberry ice cream

Mix yogurt, vanilla, and berries in the blender. Pour into tall glasses over ice cubes, or chill. Top with a big spoonful of strawberry ice cream.

PUMPKIN CARVING INSTRUCTIONS

1. Draw and cut a lid

Draw a lid on top of your pumpkin. Very carefully cut along the lines with a pumpkin carving saw (available at Halloween stores or discount stores). Angle the blade towards the center of the pumpkin. This creates a ledge to support the lid.

2. Clean and scrape

Clean out the seeds and strings with a scraper or kitchen spoon. Scrape out the inner pulp until the pumpkin wall is approximately 1-inch thick.

3. Attach the pattern

Copy your pattern, trim the pattern leaving a ½-inch border around the design. Place the pattern on the pumpkin. Press, crease, and fold the pattern so that it fits smoothly against the pumpkin. Tape the pattern to your pumpkin.

4. Transfer the pattern

Ultimately, all the black areas of the pattern will be removed from the pumpkin. Transfer the pattern by poking holes along the edges of the black areas of the pattern with a small, sharp pointed tool. You're creating a
dot-to-dot pattern on the pumpkin.

5. Carve the design

Hold the pumpkin in your lap. Hold the pumpkin carving saw like a pencil. Carefully saw dot-to-dot. Saw at a 90° angle to the pumpkin, with gentle pressure and an up and down motion. Work slowly. Pull the saw out completely and reinsert it to change the direction of the cut line. Push the cut piece out with your finger; do not pull the piece out with the blade. Remember that all the black areas of the pattern will be removed from the pumpkin.

Photocopy your pattern
before using!

Photocopy your pattern
before using!

Photocopy your pattern
before using!

Photocopy your pattern
before using!

Photocopy your pattern
before using!

Photocopy your pattern
before using!

Photocopy your pattern
before using!

Photocopy your pattern
before using!

Photocopy your pattern
before using!

Photocopy your pattern
before using!